painted calico

& découpage

Acknowledgments

Thank you to all those art and craft enthusiasts who are eager to
try something a little different.

I would like to thank Copies Now, of Norwood, South Australia for
copying my artwork with such accuracy and faithfulness to the colour.
Thank you also to Kaisercraft Pty Ltd for the supply of some of the
craftwood project pieces used in this book.

First published in 2003 by

Sally Milner Publishing Pty Ltd

PO Box 2104

Bowral NSW 2576

Australia

© Janet Eadie 2003

Design: Caroline Verity

Editing: Anne Savage

Photography: Tim Connolly

Printed in China

National Library of Australia Cataloguing-in-Publication data:

Eadie, Janet.

  Painted calico and decoupage.

  ISBN 1 86351 314 0.

  1. Calico-printing. 2. Decoupage. 3. Decoration and
  ornament. I. Title.

  746.6

painted calico
& découpage

Janet Eadie

SALLY MILNER
PUBLISHING

contents

6   Introduction

7   Painting equipment

10   Preparation of fabric

11   Painting techniques

14   Découpage equipment

16   Découpage techniques

17   Framing artwork

18   Problem solving

Projects

Butterfly

20 painted lingerie bag

23 découpage hinged box

Boats

24 painted table throw-over

27 découpage lazy susan

Dragonfly

28 painted lampshade

31 découpage terracotta dish

Seahorse

32 painted table runner

35 decoupage seahorse platter

Fish

36 painted towel border

39 découpage framed mirror

Starfish

40 painted towel border

43 découpage tissue box

Pansies

44 painted padded tea-cosy

48 découpage tray

Tulips

50 painted serviettes

53 découpage place mats

Daffodil

54 painted cushion

57 découpage planter

Iris

58 painted cushion

61 découpage greeting cards

Daisy

62 painted cushion

65 découpage papier-mâché boxes

Poppy

66 painted cushion

69 découpage document holder

Bears

70 painted flower bear with frame

73 découpage flower bearblackboard

75 découpage toy box

76 painted ballet bear with frame

80 Suppliers

introduction

This book will teach you the delightful technique of painting onto calico, with the option of colour-photocopying your artwork before it is framed or made up into a cushion or lingerie bag, for example, for use as decorative images to be applied to découpaged objects.

Painting onto calico can result in soft muted flows of colour giving an effect similar to watercolour artwork. Using calico as a base is not only economical; it is also the perfect surface for allowing soft transitions of colour to float across the design.

Your painted artwork can either be framed, or turned into more practical items to decorate your home. Full instructions are given for each project, with added directions to extend them into decoupaged projects. The method for easy découpage is also covered in this combination craft book.

For the beginner artist I have covered the simple technique of stencilling designs onto calico as a base for your artwork, then adding shading for more impact. For the more adventurous I have created more detailed projects which involve the use of shading for greater realism.

painting equipment

Calico Depending on the item to be painted, you will need to decide whether to pre-wash your calico.

If your artwork is to be framed, or for some other reason will never require washing, you can work on unwashed calico, which is much easier to paint. This means your painting will be worked over the sizing in the calico. The paint is less likely to bleed into the adjoining area which means you can work more slowly. However, if you intend to decorate a more practical item, such as the borders for the table throw-over and the towels, you will need to pre-wash the calico, as the items are likely to be washed. Artwork painted over sizing is less likely to remain permanent, as the paint will not have adhered properly to the fabric fibres.

I generally purchase good quality calico, which has more body to it. Most fabric or craft stores stock calico, so it is easy to obtain. Also, being inexpensive, you can afford the risk of a few mistakes when you first begin this technique. So be prepared to do a practice run first.

Fabric medium Where a project will require washing, you need to use fabric medium to moisten the area you are painting to allow the paint to adhere more strongly to the fibres of the calico. There are several different brands of this product.

Waterproof outline pen Where you wish for a strong outline, you can transfer the design onto your project with a waterproof pen such as a Staedtler Lumocolour 313 permanent marker in black or an Artline Drawing System pen.

Fabric paint I have used fabric paint to outline some designs design prior to painting. Fabric paint gives greater definition to a design, as it remains slightly raised. This type of paint is often referred to as 3D paint, for this reason. You can also use fabric paint to embellish your work after the water-wash and shading is complete.

Black lead pencil The use of a finely sharpened pencil to lightly outline the design will result in an outline that is almost invisible once the design is painted. You may also prefer to trace a design with pencil, before outlining it more strongly with pen or fabric paint.

Acrylic paint I have chosen to use Plaid acrylic paints for the projects in my book. There is a lovely selection of colours and the texture suits this type of artwork. However, most other types of acrylic or gouache paint will work equally well. The paint is generally diluted with water before application, but for greater impact you can apply it more solidly.

Stencils You can cut your own stencils from stencil blanks or acetate sheets. Stencil work can be enhanced by adding shading or by the use of sticker shapes, applied before painting. Some of the pre-cut stencils available from art/craft suppliers may be used to block in basic shapes, if you prefer.

Lightbox You will need to be able to trace the design onto your project. You can use any of the following methods:
1. Use a window: just tape the design to the glass and the fabric over it.
2. Use a professional lightbox.
3. A large sheet of perspex (available from plastic suppliers) can be supported at each corner to raise it above the work surface. Place a reading light underneath.
4. You could remove an unwanted picture from a large frame; leave the glass in the frame and support it above the work surface like the sheet of perspex.

Paper towel You will need this throughout the painting stage to wipe brushes on or to absorb excess moisture.

Old towel Sometimes the painting technique requires the calico to be moistened with water. An old towel placed under the calico while painting will absorb any water/paint that may seep through.

Paint brushes A selection of brushes will give you options depending on the size of area to be painted. I recommend a soft-haired 25 mm (1 in) flat brush, 12 mm (1/2 in) angle shader, and a No. 3 round brush for finer detail.

Stencil brushes A flat ended, coarse-haired stencil brush is essential for successful stencilling.

Palette For blending the paint in the process of colour floating, you will need the firm, flat surface of a white tile or ceramic plate.

Watertub A watertub with internal divisions is perfect for rinsing your brushes as well as holding clear fresh water for diluting the acrylic paint or moistening fabric surface.

Hairdryer You will need to dry the painted surface of the calico very quickly, to prevent the paint seeping into adjacent fibres. The best method of doing this is to immediately use a hairdryer to set the paint. This way the paint can be confined to separate areas of your design.

Iron If a hairdryer is unavailable, the heat from an iron will also set the paint, enabling you to proceed to the next painted area. Make sure you press with a sheet of paper towel over the calico to protect the sole-plate of the iron.

Cotton buds Cotton buds are used to soak up excess paint from areas where too much colour has been applied. It can also help to add a touch of water to such an area to dilute the paint, then soak it up with a cotton bud.

preparation of fabric

When purchasing calico for this technique, choose good quality, slightly heavier weight fabric.

As a general rule, if the item being painted is for practical use and will require washing in the future, you will need to pre-wash the calico before painting. This will enable the paint to adhere to the fabric fibres more permanently. As well as pre-washing, you will also need to use a fabric medium while painting. This is more fully described in the section below. It will be easier to iron the washed fabric smooth if the calico is slightly damp.

If the calico item is for decoration only, that is, framed artwork, then you can paint directly onto the unwashed calico and will not need to use fabric medium. This makes painting easier. You can also work more slowly on unwashed calico, as the paint will sit on top of the fabric fibres with less risk of bleeding into adjoining areas.

It is easier to work on calico cut to size, so refer to the suggested sizing for each project.

Using fabric medium I have found the easiest way of working with fabric medium where a soft, 'wash' effect is required is to mix equal parts of medium and water and paint this mix onto the area to be painted to moisten it. As you paint onto the moistened fabric, the colours bleed in soft transitions, giving an effect similar to watercolour painting. If more solid colour is being applied, you can mix the fabric medium with the paint on a palette and apply directly to the calico, following the manufacturer's instructions for the correct ratio.

Work surface Work in a well-lit area on a wide workbench with an absorbent towel under your work. Have your hairdryer close at hand, with the watertub as far away from it as possible as a safety precaution.

painting techniques

The painting method is similar for most of the projects in this book, except for the stencilled projects (the seahorse and starfish designs).

- The designs are first traced onto calico with either pencil, permanent pen or fabric paint.
- If necessary, let the outline cure before beginning the next stage of applying a paint wash.
- For a soft wash of colour, you will need to moisten a specific area with water, or a combination of fabric medium and water. Onto the moistened calico apply a paint-wash which should be allowed to seep out to the edges of the moistened area before you stop further movement by drying with a hairdryer.
- If stronger colour is required, repeat the above process.
- To shade or highlight over the top of a paint-wash, refer to the specific instructions on 'Colour floating technique' below. Sometimes it will be necessary to build up the shading by repeating the process several times until the correct depth of colour is achieved.
- Finer pen detail can be drawn in once the paintwork has dried. You can iron on the back of your artwork to make sure the fabric is completely dry.

Tracing your design You will need to trace the project design onto the calico. First of all refer to the project instructions and cut out the suggested size of calico. Use one of the following methods to trace your design onto the fabric. If using pencil first, be careful to trace only lightly, as it can be difficult to cover pencil marks with either paint or permanent pen and they will not readily wash out.

You may be fortunate enough to own a professional lightbox, in which case you can lightly trace your design onto the calico with a permanent marker or fabric paint. This will avoid using pencil first.

By taping your design underneath calico to an existing window, you can use the natural light from outside to lightly trace your design in pencil.

I prefer the option of using a large sheet of perspex or a large piece of framed glass with backing removed. Raise the perspex above the work area by supporting the four corners with equal-sized boxes or cans and place a small reading light underneath. Preferably reduce the amount of other light in the room and you will have a perfectly good lightbox to trace your design.

If using permanent pen to trace over a design, allow the ink to set overnight or, to speed up the process, iron the fabric to set the ink.

If you have used dimensional fabric paint to trace a design, you will need to allow it to cure for several hours, and, later, to avoid ironing directly onto the paint. Iron on the reverse side, if necessary.

Pen, fabric paint or pencil outline When you look through the designs in this book, you will see that those with dimensional paint outlines have more impact. The dimensional paint comes out in a thicker stream and the slightly raised effect makes it more noticeable. If you pause for too long while squeezing the tube, the paint may tend to pool up on your work. To avoid this, move at a steady pace.

The finer outline of the permanent pen will lightly define your work without detracting from the paint colours.

I have used black in most cases, but you may prefer the softer effect created by using a brown pen—or you could choose to use one of the bright-coloured dimensional paints to outline your designs. Experiment to decide which one most appeals to you.

Some of the projects have been outlined only in pencil (tulip serviettes and the two bear projects). This will give a softer appearance to your artwork and, provided the outline is done very lightly, it will be almost invisible by the time paintwork has been applied over the top.

Colour floating technique For shading and highlighting areas of your painting the following method is very important.

You will need a white tile and a good quality flat brush. I have more success using a 12 mm (1/2 in) angle shader as one side is pointed, making it easier to apply shading at the exact point where needed.

- Squeeze a small puddle of paint onto the tile or palette.
- Moisten the flat brush with water, but before using it hold the tips of the bristles to a paper towel to absorb excess water. You still need a certain amount of water on the brush to make the paint flow more softly.
- Pick up a small amount of paint on one edge only of the brush. At times you will only need a fraction of paint or the effect will be too strong.
- Blend the paint by stroking the brush several times on your palette. This will move the paint partway across the width of the brush. It is important not to move the paint all the way across the brush, as this will give you a definite stripe, rather than a soft transition of colour through to the clear water on the other side of brush.
- Use the loaded brush in short strokes, moving down the area requiring the shading. Sometimes it will be necessary to pick up a fraction more water on either side of the brush to make the shading flow smoothly.
- Reload the brush with water and paint as necessary as you go along.

découpage equipment

Project piece A variety of surfaces are suitable to decoupage – they include wood, terracotta, craftwood, papier-mâché and tin. A smooth flat surface will make it easier to apply your design, so choose your project base carefully according to your level of decoupage experience.

Colour photocopied design Commercial colour-copy stores can professionally copy your artwork. You can have your designs enlarged or reduced or mirror-imaged to give variation to your work. Home scanners can also be used for smaller designs.

Scissors Choose small, pointed scissors to accurately cut fine detail on your copied artwork.

Glue (clear gum) This water-based glue is non-toxic and is available from most newsagents.
It has a thick consistency, giving good adhesion, and dries clear.

Decoupage rollers These are essential for a smooth finish to your glued design. Rollers are available from art and craft outlets and come in several widths. The rubber-coated roller will glide smoothly over the image, pushing out excess glue and air which might otherwise remain trapped underneath the image – definitely worth purchasing.

Paper sealer (varnish) I have had great success sealing the photocopied image with the same water-based varnish used for finishing the project. This eliminates the purchase of an extra product.

Basecoat paint Generally two coats of white undercoat are applied to the project surface prior to the final basecoat colour. This ensures a clearer, more vibrant finish. Most acrylic or gouache paints will be suitable as a basecoat. Avoid using gloss paint as a basecoat, as it repels glue.

Fine sandpaper Between basecoats you will need to smooth the surface by lightly sanding with fine-grade sandpaper. Some terracotta surfaces will need to be sanded prior to basecoating to remove bumps.

Soft cloth (dampened) Used to wipe over the glued image to remove excess glue from around the edges.

Craft knife The fine, pointed blade of a craft knife enables fine detail to be cut on internal areas of the paper images.
A self-healing cutting mat is used as a base.

Brushes or foam applicators Used to paint the background colour on the project and to apply glue to the back of the photocopied image. The coarser the hair in the brush, the more textured the paintwork will appear. Foam applicators are inexpensive and give a fine appearance when used for basecoating. They also come in several widths.

Waterbased varnish I use Cabot's Crystal Clear waterbased varnish, which is available from most hardware stores.

Wood-filler Check your project before basecoating for any nail-holes or gaps in joins. Apply wood-filler to the imperfections and when dry sand lightly.

découpage techniques

Use waterbased varnish to seal the front of your photocopied image prior to gluing. This will help protect the paper surface, as well as making the paper less likely to wrinkle when the glue is applied. There are various sealers available but I have found that the waterbased varnish used to finish the projects works very well over the photocopies.

If using a wooden or craftwood project piece, fill any holes or gaps with wood-filler before painting.

Apply several coats of basecoat paint to the piece to give a good even coverage, allowing to dry properly and sanding lightly between coats.

Apply a light coat of sealer or varnish to the painted surface prior to applying decoupage. This will stop the glue from soaking into the paint, giving better adhesion of your design.

Once the sealed paper has dried, cut around the required shapes with very sharp, fine-pointed scissors and check their arrangement on the project before applying any glue. When you are satisfied, apply a complete coverage of glue to the back of each element of the paper design and glue into place. Use the decoupage roller or your fingertips to smooth out any air-bubbles or excess glue from underneath the design.

Wipe away any excess glue with a dampened soft cloth and allow the project to dry for 24 hours.

To complete your project you can apply several coats of gloss or satin finish varnish.

framing artwork

You may prefer to frame your own artwork as an alternative to having it professionally done. The type of frame with metal press-down clips at the back is much easier to work with than the type where you have to use staples.

Your artwork will look more attractive if it is backed with quilt wadding. Cut the wadding to fit the size of internal frame area. Trim the artwork, making sure you leave enough calico to allow you to fold the sides securely to the back. Position the artwork over the wadding and backing board. Fold the edges of the calico over to the back and secure with strong masking tape.

Insert the artwork into the frame and press the metal clips into place.

problem solving

Painting on calico

- If you find the pen or fabric paint outline begins to smudge when moisture is applied, this means you have not waited long enough for the outline to dry properly. Make sure you are using a waterproof outliner.

- If paint begins to seep outside the design outline you can soften the effect by immediately wiping with a damp cloth. Blot with another dry cloth to avoid further spreading. This may, however, cause a smudged effect.

- Paint too dark? This is due to applying too strong a colour in the original water-wash. It can be softened before it has time to dry by adding a few drops of water to the dark area and blotting with a dry cloth or cotton bud. Repeat until a softer colour is achieved.

- Painted items fade when washed? Failure to use a fabric medium, which should lock the paint permanently into the fibres of the fabric, may result in fading. Heat setting the paint with an iron will also help to keep the artwork permanent.

- Stripes in your shading rather than a soft transition of colour? This is because the flat brush has not been correctly loaded with water and paint to create a soft blend. Reread the instructions under 'Colour floating technique', and practise on some scrap calico before moving onto another project.

Decoupage

- You may find your paper designs have not attached securely to the project surface. Sometimes this will be noticeable at the edges of the images. This may be caused by not enough glue being applied to the back of the photocopied image. To correct this, use the tip of a fine round brush or the tip of a pin to push extra glue under the offending area. Any excess glue that is pressed out from underneath can be wiped away with a soft damp cloth.

- If the photocopied image is easily rubbed off in the gluing process, this could be because the image was not properly sealed prior to cutting out. Make sure varnish or sealer is applied to the whole of each image to protect the design.

- Trapped air-bubbles under image? Before the glue has dried, tilt your project against a good light to assess whether there are any pockets of trapped air. If there are, prick each one with a fine needle and gently work the air out with your fingertips or the decoupage roller.

- Areas lifting up? This may be due to insufficient glue underneath the image. You will need to carefully cut a small incision next to this area using a sharp craft knife. Push extra glue underneath the image and use the decoupage roller or your fingertips to press down firmly. If the cut is visible it can be camouflaged with a little paint applied with a fine brush.

- Streaky varnish? Always allow 24 hours for the glued images to dry before varnishing. Use a soft-haired brush and long even strokes when applying the varnish. Read the instruction label carefully and apply within recommended temperatures.

butterfly

MATERIALS

Calico,
40 x 60 cm (16 x 24 in)

Cream satin,
40 x 60 cm (16 x 24 in)

12 small pearl beads

Beading needle

Soft wadding to pad the bag

Plaid FolkArt paint:
Light Fuchsia, Purple,
Periwinkle, Light Periwinkle,
Purple Lilac

Plaid fabric medium

Brushes:
12 mm (1/2 in) angle shader,
5 mm (1/4 in) angle shader,
No. 4 round

Black Artline pen No. 5

Tile for palette

Watertub

Hairdryer

Paper towel

Old absorbent towel

Lightbox
or other tracing system

METHOD

Wash calico once and press to remove creases.

Begin by cutting out shape of lingerie bag and fold at marked points to gauge where design should be drawn on.

Outline the butterfly design in black waterproof pen and allow to dry 12 hours, or set with the heat of iron.

Half butterfly Work on the top two wings of upper section of bag first. Moisten internal areas of butterfly wings with fabric medium and while still moist, pick up Purple Lilac on 12 mm (1/2 in) shader brush and float colour across this section. Dilute some Light Fuchsia with a fraction of water to an ink-like consistency. Pick up on the tip of the round brush and use this to paint in the wing detail. If the fabric underneath is still a little moist, the colour will bleed slightly, giving a softer appearance. Halt the process with heat from the hairdryer.

Next, deepen shading nearest centre body with Periwinkle, using the 12 mm (1/2 in) angle shader. On the outer portion of wings, apply a base of fabric medium and while this is still moist, paint in a wash of Light Periwinkle. Add extra shading using Periwinkle. While this area is still moist, apply dots of Purple (make an ink-like consistency first by adding a few drops of water). Halt the spread of the purple dots by applying heat from the hairdryer.

Body Apply a layer of fabric medium to calico in this area. Use the 5 mm (1/4 in) shader to float Periwinkle around the outer edges of body.

Then run a line of Purple Lilac down centre. If base underneath is still a little moist, this will soften the effect.

Full butterfly Repeat the process for the complete butterfly, worked on the lower section of lingerie bag. Float some Purple paint under the top wings as a shadow, to make the wings more defined.

When completely dry, use the Artline pen to draw in antennae for both butterflies.

lingerie bag
PAINTED CALICO PROJECT

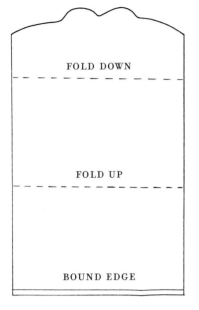

pattern for flap of lingerie bag for actual size template, enlarge to 200%

lingerie bag *(continued)*

FOLD DOWN

FOLD UP

BOUND EDGE

construction of lingerie bag

Making up bag Cut wadding, lining and painted calico to correct shape, leaving a 12 mm (1/2 in) seam allowance.

Lay right side of painted calico onto lining with wadding on top. Stitch around scalloped edge and both sides. Be careful to stitch a fraction away from the painted edge of butterfly wing so when the bag is turned right side out, the seam won't hide the black outline.

Layer seams and nick the curved edges of scalloped section. Turn the bag right side out and press. At this stage it will be a long rectangle with the straight edge unfinished.

To neaten this unfinished edge, you will need to cut a 25 mm (1 in) wide strip of satin and stitch in place.

To complete bag construction, fold up at lower edge, right sides facing together. Stitch and overlock edges. Turn the bag right side out. Stitch small pearl beads at the tips of the antennae and along the scalloped edge.

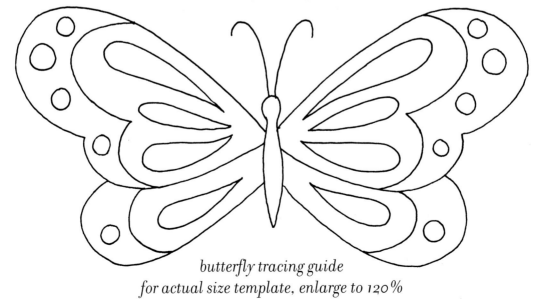

butterfly tracing guide
for actual size template, enlarge to 120%

butterfly
hinged box

MATERIALS

Small domed box,
15 x 10 x 5.5 cm
(6 x 4 x 2 1/4 in)

Plaid FolkArt paint:
Light Fuchsia,
Light Periwinkle, Purple Lilac

Plaid FolkArt Artist's
Pigment: Titanium White

Plaid Dimensional Fabric
Paint: Plum Pearl

Colour photocopy of
painted butterfly,
reduced to approx. 80%

Wide basecoating brush

Black Artline pen No. 5

Decoupage glue

Decoupage roller

Soft cloth, moistened

Scissors

Sandpaper, fine grade

Waterbased varnish

METHOD

Basecoat the entire box with Titanium White and allow to dry. Sand lightly. Squeeze lines of Light Fuchsia, Light Periwinkle and Purple Lilac paint onto one surface of the box at random — approximately 20 mm (3/4 in) apart. Immediately spray with a mist of water, then with the basecoating brush blend the paints to a soft streaky appearance. Repeat this process over each side of the box, working one side at a time.

The inside of the box can be painted one straight colour. Allow all paintwork to dry. Paint top of lid with a coat of varnish to seal before applying decoupage.

Decoupage butterfly Seal the top of the photocopied butterfly design with a thin coat of varnish. Allow to dry, then cut out the shape, omitting the antennae, as these are drawn in later. Apply glue to the back of butterfly and stick in place. Use decoupage roller to remove any excess glue and trapped air. Wipe surface clean with a soft moist cloth.

Allow to dry overnight before painting with several coats of varnish. It is best to varnish at this stage, before the dimensional paint antennae are applied.

Antennae Use the Artline pen to draw in the antennae and squeeze a small bead of Plum Pearl dimensional paint at the tip of each one.

boats

MATERIALS

Calico,
60 x 115 cm wide
(24 x 45 in)

Blue net,
80 cm (32 in) square

Plaid FolkArt paint:
Azure Blue, Coastal Blue,
Light Blue, Fresh Foliage,
Teal, Bright Green,
Brilliant Blue

Plaid fabric medium

Brushes: round No. 1,
25 mm (1 in) flat,
12 mm (1/2 in) angle shader

Black Artline pen No. 8

Tile for palette

Watertub

Hairdryer

Paper towel

Old absorbent towel

Pins

Lightbox
or other tracing system

METHOD

Wash calico once and press to remove creases.

Cut calico into four 14 cm (5 1/2 in) wide strips, two measuring 105 cm
(41 1/2 in) long and two measuring 82 cm (32 1/2 in) long. Join the calico to
the blue net as a border, using square corners.

Overlock the outside edges of the calico, press under a 12 mm (1/2 in) hem and
stitch. Using pins, work out the even placement of three boats along each strip.
Use a lightbox to trace the boats onto the calico with the Artline pen. Next,
referring to the photograph for guidance, draw in three wavy lines, joining them
up at each corner to form the water area. Allow the ink to set overnight, or use
the heat of an iron to set it.

Boat 1

Sails First moisten the area to be painted with fabric medium and while still
wet, paint entire sail with a wash of Coastal Blue. Allow to dry and intensify the
colour on left-hand side by floating Azure Blue. On right-hand side use a float of
Brilliant Blue. While the sail area is still moist, apply spots of Brilliant Blue and
halt the bleeding process with heat from the hairdryer.

Flag and hull First apply fabric medium, and then a wash of Fresh Foliage.
Shade with a mix of Teal and Bright Green (1:1).

Boat 2

Sails First moisten the area to be painted with fabric medium and while still
wet, paint entire sail with a wash of Fresh Foliage. Allow to dry and intensify the
colour on right-hand side by floating with a mix of Teal and Bright Green (1:1).
While the sail area is still moist, use the fine round brush to paint in stripes with
a mix of Teal and Bright Green (1:1) and halt the bleeding process with heat
from the hairdryer.

Flag and hull First apply fabric medium and then a wash of Azure Blue.
Shade with Brilliant Blue.

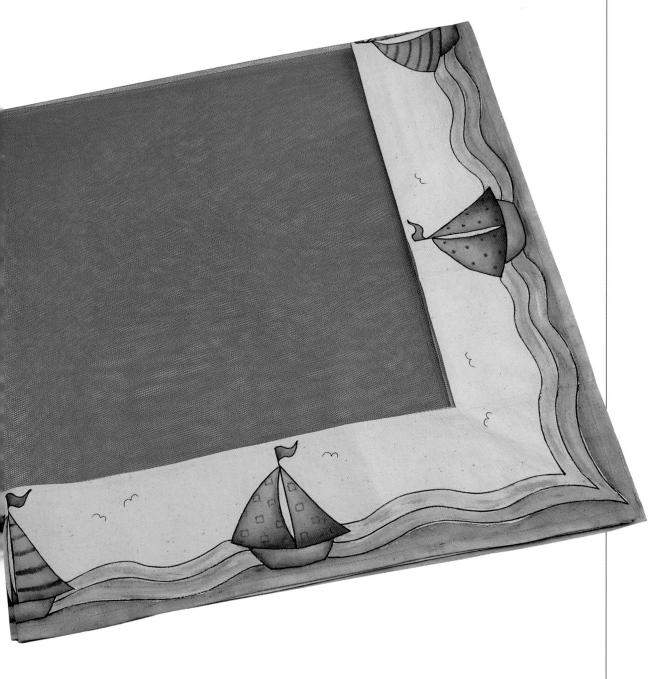

Boat 3

Sails First moisten the area to be painted with fabric medium and while still wet, paint entire sail with a wash of Coastal Blue. Allow to dry and intensify the colour on left-hand side by floating Azure Blue. On right-hand side use a float of Brilliant Blue. While the sail area is still moist, paint in small squares using Brilliant Blue and halt the bleeding process with heat from the hairdryer.

Flag and hull First apply fabric medium and then a wash of Fresh Foliage. Shade with a mix of Teal and Bright Green (1:1).

Water It will be easier to mix fabric medium into the paint before painting the bands of colour. Remember to dry each area before beginning another, otherwise the next paint application will bleed into the first area. To intensify the colour in some areas, pick up extra paint on the edge of your brush and apply to the moist calico.

Begin at base and paint with Azure Blue.

The middle band is painted with Coastal Blue and the upper water area is Light Blue.

To complete, draw in simple bird shapes at random on background sky area with the Artline pen.

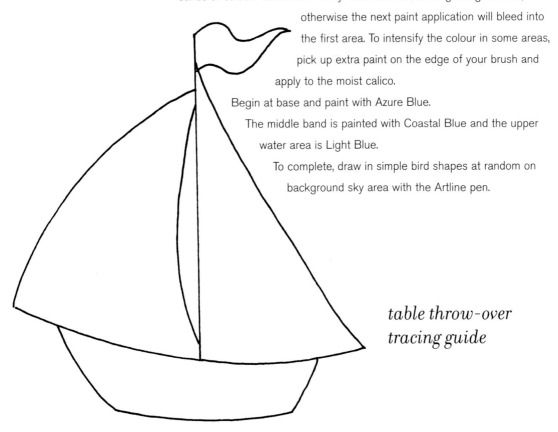

table throw-over
tracing guide

boats
lazy susan

MATERIALS

Craftwood lazy susan, approx. 40 cm (16 in) diameter

Plaid FolkArt paint: Coastal Blue, Azure Blue, Brilliant Blue

Plaid FolkArt Artists' Pigment: Titanium White

6 colour photocopies of boats: 2 of each boat, enlarged at 110%

25 mm (1 in) basecoating brush

25 mm (1 in) foam applicator

Black Artline pen No. 8

Chalk pencil

Decoupage glue

Decoupage roller

Soft cloth, moistened

Scissors

Waterspray

Sandpaper, fine grade

Waterbased varnish

METHOD

Unscrew the base from the lazy susan before painting. Basecoat all areas of the base and the turntable with two coats of Titanium White and allow to dry. Sand lightly after final coat. Sit the top of the lazy susan back on the base to allow it to turn while you are painting the topcoat. Squeeze a swirl of white in centre, outside this a swirl of Coastal Blue, outside this a swirl of Azure Blue. Spray with a light mist of water and slowly turn the lazy susan, using the wide basecoating brush to blend the colours together. Allow to dry before repeating this on the reverse of the turntable.

Use Brilliant Blue on the flat edge of the foam applicator to paint the outer edges of the turntable and the base. Allow all paintwork to dry.

Use the chalk pencil to draw a wavy line border approximately 5 cm (2 in) in from outer edge of the turntable. Draw over this with the Artline pen and allow to dry overnight. Paint inside border with a float of Azure Blue with more shading on lower edge of border. Paint top of turntable with a coat of varnish to seal before applying decoupage.

Decoupage Seal the tops of the photocopied boats with a thin coat of varnish. Allow to dry, then cut out each shape. Before gluing onto the upper surface of the turntable, work out the best placement, then apply glue to the backs and attach to project surface. Use the decoupage roller to remove any excess glue and trapped air. Wipe surface clean with a soft moist cloth. Allow to dry overnight before painting with several coats of varnish.

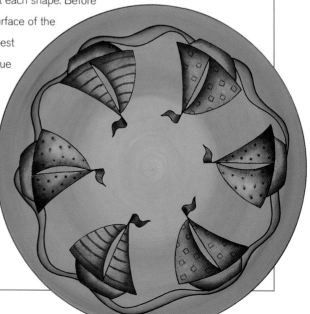

dragonfly

MATERIALS

Calico lampshade, approx.
36 cm diam. x 25 cm deep
(14 in diam. x 10 in deep)

Lamp base
in complementary colour

Plaid FolkArt paint:
Teal Green, Sky Blue,
Turquoise, Patina,
Azure Blue, Coastal Blue

Metallic paint: Champagne

Plaid Dimensional Fabric
Paint: Peacock Sparkle, Aqua
Glitter, Blue Ocean Glitter

Brushes:
12 mm (1/2 in) angle shader,
5 mm (1/4 in) angle shader

Black Artline pen No. 3

Tile for palette

Watertub

Hairdryer

Paper towel

Old absorbent towel

Sticky-tape

METHOD

Practice on a piece of scrap calico before moving onto the lampshade. Your best practice dragonfly in the No. 3 colour scheme can be used to make the photocopy for the decoupage dragonfly for the terracotta dish.

Work out correct placement to evenly space nine dragonflies around the base of the lampshade. You can do this by placing some sticky-tape at each point. Use the lamp itself as the light source to allow you to trace the dragonflies onto the shade using the Artline pen.

Allow the ink to set overnight.

Painting Using the 12 mm (1/2 in) angle shader, paint in a coat of Champagne on the lower wings. Float Sky Blue at the base of each body segment and build up stronger shading using Teal Green.

Each dragonfly is painted in the same manner, shading the upper wing areas with the lighter colour and using the deeper colour to shade the lower wings. When wing area is dry, brush a layer of sparkle or glitter fabric paint on the upper wing areas, squeeze on two beads of fabric paint in the corresponding colour for the eyes, and draw in a short line on upper wing area using the same fabric paint, following the photograph for guidance.

Dragonfly 1 Patina (upper wing), Turquoise (lower wing), Aqua Glitter fabric paint (upper wing highlight, eyes and line near wingtip).

Dragonfly 2 Coastal Blue (upper wing), Azure Blue (lower wing), and Peacock Sparkle fabric paint (upper wing highlight, eyes and line near wingtip).

Dragonfly 3 Use Sky Blue (upper wing), Teal Green (lower wing), and Blue Ocean Glitter fabric paint (upper wing highlight, eyes and line near wingtip). Allow the paint to dry overnight before placing the lampshade on the base.

lampshade

PAINTED CALICO PROJECT

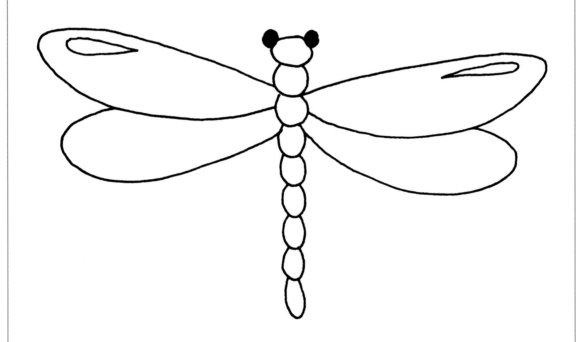

dragonfly tracing guide
for actual size template, reduce to 80%

dragonfly
terracotta dish

MATERIALS

Terracotta dish,
16 cm (6 1/2 in) square

Plaid FolkArt paint:
Teal Green, French Vanilla

Plaid fabric paint:
Blue Ocean Glitter

Colour photocopy of
dragonfly in No. 3 colour
scheme, enlarged to 138%

Basecoating brush

Varnishing brush

Decoupage glue

Decoupage roller

Soft cloth, moistened

Scissors

Sandpaper, fine grade

Waterbased varnish

METHOD

Basecoat the top surface of the terracotta dish with two coats of French Vanilla and the undersurface with two coats of Teal Green. When dry, apply a coat of varnish to the top surface to seal it prior to gluing on the design.

Decoupage Seal the front of the photocopied dragonfly with varnish. When dry, carefully cut out the shape. Apply glue to the back of design and press in place with fingertips. Use the decoupage roller to remove any excess glue and trapped air. Wipe away excess glue with a soft moistened cloth. Allow the glue to dry, then paint several layers of varnish over the front and back of dish to protect the surface.

Add two beads of Blue Ocean Glitter fabric paint for the dragonfly's eyes.

seahorse

MATERIALS

Calico,
120 x 30 cm (48 x 12 in)

Stencil blank
or A4 acetate sheet

Plaid FolkArt paint:
Patina, Fresh Foliage, Purple
Lilac, Light Periwinkle

Plaid fabric medium

4 stencil brushes:
12 mm (1/2 in)

12 mm (1/2 in) angle shader

Cutting blade and mat

Tile for palette

Hairdryer

Paper towelling

Circle stickers: 10 mm (3/8 in)
and 15 mm (5/8 in) diameter

Sticky-tape

Flat-based pens
(or fine dowelling) to print
border: 12 mm (1/2 in) and 10
mm (3/8 in) diameter

Old absorbent towel

Pins

METHOD

Wash calico once and press well to remove creases.

Begin by overlocking all edges of the calico and pressing under a 25 mm (1 in) hem. Stitch in place.

Making stencil First trace the seahorse pattern onto paper and lay it under the stencil blank/acetate, then fix the two firmly together. Use the cutting blade to cut out the seahorse shape. Use pins to mark out even spacing for the four seahorses along the centre of the table runner and sticky-tape the stencil in place. Use the circle stickers at random within the stencilled design to block off areas which will be painted in later. Alternate the size of stickers for each stencilled seahorse.

Stencilling The colours used are:

Seahorse 1 Patina with Purple Lilac spots.

Seahorse 2 Fresh Foliage with Light Periwinkle spots.

Seahorse 3 Purple Lilac with Fresh Foliage spots.

Seahorse 4 Light Periwinkle with Patina spots.

Squeeze a small puddle of paint onto your palette and mix fabric medium into the paint, following the manufacturer's directions. Pick up some paint on the stencil brush. Pad the brush up and down on the palette, several times, to work the paint into the body of brush before stencilling. Using a padding motion, apply paint to the fabric inside the stencil shape. When complete, carefully lift off the stencil and the stickers. Wipe all paint off the surface of the stencil before reversing its direction for the next seahorse. Repeat for each seahorse. Allow the paint to dry.

table runner

PAINTED CALICO PROJECT

table runner *(continued)*

To paint in the spots, first paint fabric medium over each circle within one seahorse. While this is still wet, apply a wash of paint in the appropriate colour, strengthening the colour around the edge of each circle by floating on extra colour which has been blended onto the edge of your angled shader brush. Allow the paint to dry overnight, or iron to set.

Border Use the base of the 12 mm (¹⁄₂ in) pen to print the borders at the short ends of the table runner in the colours used on the seahorses, applying the colours in random order. Mix some fabric medium with paint before printing. Repeat along the long sides using the smaller pen.

seahorse tracing guide
for actual size template, enlarge to 120%

seahorse
oval platter

MATERIALS

Craftwood oval platter,
43 x 28 cm (17 x 11 in)

Plaid FolkArt paint:
Fresh Foliage, Turquoise

Plaid FolkArt Artists'
Pigment: Titanium White

Colour photocopies of
Seahorse 1 and Seahorse 4,
copied at 100%

[[designer, confirm colours
according to photo and
colour guide attached to
diagram 5]]

Basecoating brush

25 mm (1 in) foam
applicator

Tile for palette

Varnishing brush

Decoupage glue

Soft cloth, moistened

Scissors

Waterspray

Sandpaper, fine grade

Flat-based pen,
10 mm (³/₈ in) diameter

Waterbased varnish

METHOD

Basecoat both sides of platter in two coats of Titanium White. Sand lightly when dry. Paint a topcoat of Fresh Foliage. Print spots of Turquoise around outer border using the flat base of the pen. Paint a Turquoise border around rim using the flat side of the 25 mm (1 in) wide foam applicator.
Allow to dry and apply a light coat of varnish over the top surface.

Decoupage Seal the front of the colour-photocopied seahorse with varnish and when dry, carefully cut out the shape. Apply glue to the back of design and press in place with fingertips. Use the decoupage roller to remove any excess glue and trapped air. Wipe away excess glue with a soft moistened cloth. Wipe the surface clean with a soft moistened cloth and allow glue to dry.
Paint several layers of varnish over platter to protect the surface.

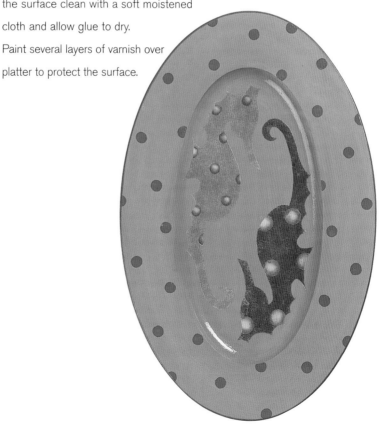

fish

MATERIALS

Blue handtowel,
approx. 46 cm (18 in) wide

Calico,
approx. 50 x 12 cm
(20 x 5 in)

Plaid FolkArt paint:
Light Periwinkle, True Blue

Plaid FolkArt Artists'
Pigment: Titanium White

Plaid fabric medium

Brushes: 12 mm (1/2 in)
angle shader, No. 2 liner

Black Artline pen No. 8

Tile for palette

Watertub

Hairdryer

Paper towel

Toothpick

Old absorbent towel

Lightbox
or other tracing system

METHOD

Wash calico once and press well to remove creases.

Pin design underneath calico and place over a light source to trace the design using the Artline pen. Allow to set for approximately twelve hours, or iron over the top to set the ink before painting.

Fish 1 To make the paint colourfast, you will need to apply a layer of fabric medium over the area to be painted. Begin painting by shading around the outer edges of the fish using True Blue. To do this, squeeze a puddle of True Blue paint onto your tile. Moisten the 12 mm (1/2 in) flat brush in water and hold onto paper towel to remove the excess moisture. Pick up a small amount of paint on one edge of the brush and blend on tile to move paint partway across bristles. Use this technique to build up intensity of colour around the fish (refer to photograph for guidance). By moistening the entire body of the fish, but only painting around the edge, you will achieve a soft blending of colour that remains lighter in the middle.

While calico is still moist you can add fine spots of paint diluted with a little water to an ink-like consistency (using No. 2 liner brush). These will bleed slightly out of shape, at which point you will need to halt the spread of paint by drying with hairdryer.

When paint has dried, use the Artline pen to draw in the eye, then add a fine dot of Titanium White using the end of a toothpick.

Fish 2 As before, start by applying a layer of fabric medium over the area to be painted. Next, begin to shade around the outer edges of fish with Light Periwinkle, using the same technique as for Fish 1.

Refer to the photograph for guidance.

While calico is still moist you can paint in the zig-zag stripes down body, using paint diluted with a few drops of water, with the No. 2 liner brush. These will bleed slightly out of shape, when you will again need to halt the spread of paint by drying with the hairdryer.

Add stronger shading around base of body, inner fin and inner tail areas using a wash of True Blue.

handtowel

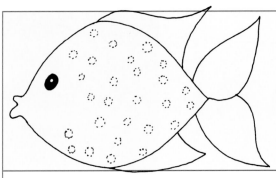

FISH 1

FISH 2

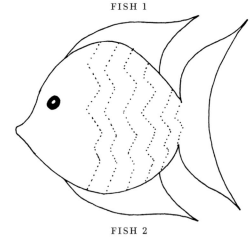

FISH 3

When paint has dried, use the Artline pen to draw in the eye and add a fine dot of Titanium White with a toothpick.

Fish 3 As before, start by applying a layer of fabric medium over the area to be painted. Next, begin to shade around the outer edges of fish with True Blue, using the same technique as for Fish 1.
Refer to the photograph for guidance.
While calico is still moist, shade one edge of each of the scalloped stripes with a stronger wash of True Blue. Halt the spread of paint by drying with the hairdryer.
When paint has dried, use the Artline pen to draw in the eye and add a fine dot of Titanium White with a toothpick.

Fish 4 As before, start by applying a layer of fabric medium over the area to be painted. Next, begin to shade around the outer edges of fish with Light Periwinkle, using the same technique as for Fish 1. Refer to the photograph for guidance.
While calico is still moist, paint in stripes with a wash of colour, alternating between Light Periwinkle and True Blue. Alternate the colours for the stripes on the tail as well. Halt the spread of paint by drying with the hairdryer. Shade around the outer edges of the fish with True Blue.
When paint has dried, use the Artline pen to draw in the eye and add a fine dot of Titanium White with a toothpick.

Making up the border
Once the paint has dried, iron the calico flat and press the edges under to fit the dimensions of towel. Pin in place, and using matching thread machine-stitch to the towel.

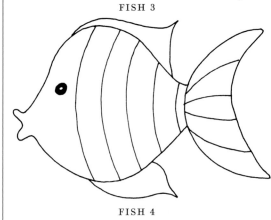

FISH 4

fish tracing guides
for actual size template, enlarge to 150%

fish
framed mirror

DÉCOUPAGE PROJECT

MATERIALS

Wooden mirror, approx. 38 cm (15 in) square

Plaid FolkArt paint: Skintone

Plaid FolkArt Artists' Pigment: Titanium White

Colour photocopies of fish (choose sizes randomly):

2 enlarged to 185%

3 enlarged to 150%

4 at 100%

Coarse-haired basecoating brush

Decoupage glue

Decoupage roller

Soft cloth, moistened

Scissors

Scalpel knife

Waterspray

Sandpaper, fine grade

Waterbased varnish

METHOD

Remove mirror from frame and set aside.

Apply enough coats of Skintone paint to achieve a good coverage over the entire mirror. Sand lightly between coats.

Over the final coat, use Titanium White on the tip of the coarse-haired brush to dry-brush a linen-grain effect on parts of frame. When dry, seal the surface with a light coat of varnish prior to gluing designs.

Decoupage Seal front of photocopied designs with varnish and when dry, carefully cut around shapes. To test arrangement prior to gluing, lay these over the mirror frame, using the photograph as a guide. At this stage, don't trim the designs where they overlap frame. It is easier to glue as a whole and trim off later when glue has dried.

Apply glue to the back of each design and press in place with fingertips. Use the decoupage roller to remove any excess glue and trapped air. Wipe away excess glue with a soft moistened cloth. When all designs are glued in place, wipe the entire surface of frame again with soft moistened cloth. Allow to dry overnight. Lay the mirror upside down and use scalpel knife to trim excess paper away from edges of frame. Paint or spray a protective coat of varnish over frame.

starfish

MATERIALS

Turquoise handtowel, approx. 46 cm (18 in) wide

Calico, approx. 50 x 12 cm (20 x 5 in)

Plaid FolkArt paint: Azure Blue, Turquoise, Lavender

Plaid fabric medium

Stencil blank or A4 acetate sheet

Cutting blade and mat

3 x stencil brushes: 12 mm (1/2 in)

Star stickers (available from stationers): 15 mm (5/8in) and 25 mm (1 in) wide

Sticky-tape

Tile for palette

Hairdryer

Paper towel

Old absorbent towel

METHOD

Wash calico once and press well to remove creases.

Making stencil First trace the starfish pattern onto paper and lay it under the stencil blank/acetate, then fix the two firmly together. Use a cutting blade to cut the starfish stencil.

Stencilling Work out even spacings along the calico strip for the five starfish, and sticky-tape the stencil in place for the first one. Referring to the photograph for guidance, place the star stickers at random within the stencil. Refer to the photograph for suggested colours, making sure you use a separate stencil brush for each paint colour. On your tile squeeze a puddle of paint and mix some fabric medium into it. Pick up some paint on the stencil brush. Pad this up and down on tile to work the paint up into the bristles before commencing the stencilling.

Lift the stencil carefully from the fabric and clean it before moving on to the next starfish.

Allow the paint to dry completely before removing the star stickers.

Making up border Once the paint has dried, iron the calico flat and press the edges under to fit the dimensions of towel. Pin in place, and using matching thread machine-stitch to the towel.

handtowel

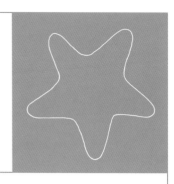

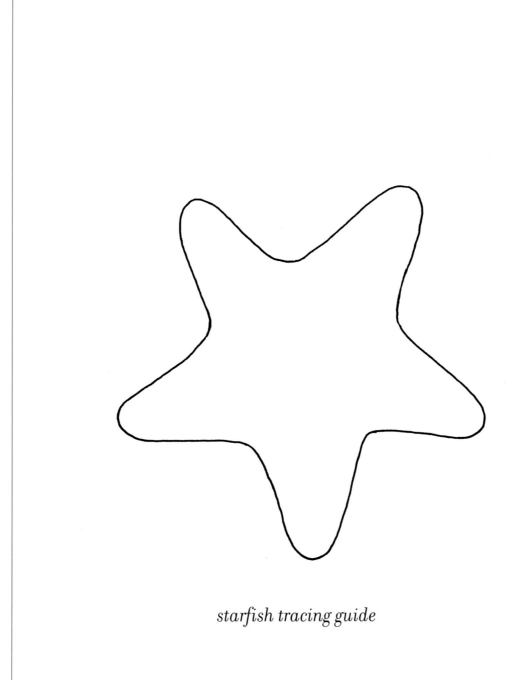

starfish tracing guide

starfish
tissue-box

DÉCOUPAGE PROJECT

MATERIALS

Wooden tissue-box, approx. 12.5 x 12 x 13 cm (5 x 4 3/4 x 5 1/4 in)

Plaid FolkArt paint: Azure Blue, Turquoise

Plaid FolkArt Artists' Pigment: Titanium White

5 colour photocopies of starfish, all enlarged at 135%

Basecoating brush

Varnishing brush

Decoupage glue

Decoupage roller

Soft cloth, moistened

Scissors

Scalpel knife

Spray waterbottle

Sandpaper, fine grade

Waterbased varnish

METHOD

Apply enough coats of Titanium White paint to achieve a good coverage over all sides of tissue-box. Sand lightly between coats.

To create the washed background you will need to work on one side at a time. Spray with a light mist of water and apply thin stripes of Azure Blue and Turquoise, squeezed straight from tube at random — about 20 mm (3/4 in) apart. Blend these slightly, then again spray lightly with water and allow to dribble downwards. When you are satisfied with the effect, lay the box so the painted surface is horizontal, leaving it until the paint has dried. Repeat on all sides. When all surfaces are painted and completely dry, seal with a light coat of varnish prior to gluing on the designs.

Decoupage Seal front of photocopied starfish with varnish. When dry, carefully cut around each one. To test arrangement prior to gluing, lay the shapes in position, using the photograph as a guide. At this stage, don't cut out the circle on the top of tissue-box. It is easier to glue the design as a whole, then cut out the circle with a scalpel knife when glue has dried.

Apply glue to the back of each starfish and press in place with fingertips. Use the decoupage roller to remove any excess glue and trapped air. Wipe away excess glue with a soft moistened cloth. When all designs are glued in place, wipe the entire surface of the tissue-box again with soft moistened cloth. Allow to dry overnight. Apply several coats of varnish to protect the surface.

pansy

MATERIALS

Calico,
28 x 40 cm (11 x 16 in)

Yellow lining fabric,
28 x 45 cm (11 x 17 ³/4 in)

Soft wadding to pad tea-cosy

1 skein matching
blue stranded cotton
embroidery thread

1 skein matching
yellow stranded cotton
embroidery thread

Plaid FolkArt paint:
Lemon Custard, Dark Brown,
True Blue, Night Sky,
Fresh Foliage

Plaid FolkArt Artists'
Pigment: Turners Yellow

Plaid fabric medium

Brushes: 12 mm (¹/2 in)
angle shader, 5 mm (¹/4 in)
angle shader, No. 4 round

Black Artline pen No. 3

Tile for palette

Watertub

Hairdryer

Paper towel

Old absorbent towel

Lightbox
or other tracing system

METHOD

Wash calico once and press well to remove creases. Only one side will be painted. Fold the calico in half to gauge the correct placement of the design, but don't cut it, as the tea-cosy is worked as one piece.

Trace the outlines of the pansy design in the black Artline pen. Don't add the fine line details on the lower petals at this stage. Allow to dry for twelve hours, or set with the heat of the iron.

Painting The pansies are begun by painting in a layer of fabric medium on each outlined section being worked and while this is still wet applying a soft colour wash. The bleeding process is halted with a hairdryer. Refer to photograph for guidance.

Pansy 1 Work one petal at a time. Paint fabric medium onto back petal, then apply a wash of True Blue. Deepen shading at inner corner by shading with Night Sky. Dry paint well before repeating process on second back petal and drying paintwork. For the two middle petals, apply a base of fabric medium and over this a wash of True Blue. Shade the area just behind the front petal with a stronger application of True Blue and dry well. Paint in a layer of fabric medium onto the front petal, then a wash of True Blue, leaving some of the area paler in colour for a slight highlight. Float some True Blue shading and Night Sky shading around the lower portion of this petal and dry well.

Pansy 2 Use the same colours as for Pansy 1, but give this pansy a slightly different appearance.

Pansy 3 Work one petal at a time. Paint fabric medium onto back petal, then apply a wash of Lemon Custard. Deepen shading at inner corner and behind middle petal with a float of Turners Yellow and a soft float of Dark Brown. Dry paint well before repeating process on second back petal and drying paintwork. For the two middle petals, apply a base of fabric medium and over this a wash of Lemon Custard. Shade the area just behind the front petal with a float of Turners Yellow and a soft float of Dark Brown. and dry well. Paint in a layer of fabric medium onto the front petal, then a wash of Lemon Custard, leaving some of the area paler in colour for a slight highlight. Float Lemon Custard shading around the lower portion of this petal. Dry well.

tea-cosy

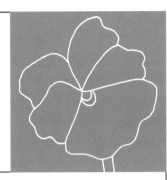

tea-cosy *(continued)*

Pansy 4 Use the same colours as for Pansy 1, but give this pansy a slightly different appearance.

Pansy 5 Use the same colours as for Pansy 3, but give this pansy a slightly different appearance.

Centres and lines The centre of each pansy is painted with a dot of Fresh Foliage, using the tip of the round brush. The area just below this is painted with Turners Yellow.
Iron your paintwork dry before using the Artline pen to draw in the fine line details on the middle and lower petals, referring to the photograph for guidance.

Leaves and stems Paint the stems with fabric medium and, while still wet, paint in a wash of Fresh Foliage. Paint a wash of fabric medium onto the leaf area and, while still wet, paint in a wash of Fresh Foliage. The shading on the leaves is created by floating a stronger application of Fresh Foliage in a scalloped effect on the lower halves of the leaves.

Cord ties For each tie, cut two 50 cm (20 in) lengths of stranded cotton, one in each colour. Tie a knot at one end and fix that end to something like a hook. Twist the other end until the cord doubles back on itself, forming a rope-like effect. Hold the two ends evenly together and tie another knot 20 mm (3/4 in) above first. Cut ends evenly to form tassel.

Assembling tea-cosy Before constructing the tea-cosy, you will need to hem one edge of each half of yellow lining. Fold over raw edge on one long side of each half and press, turn up again to form a 20 mm (3/4 in) hem.
Lay the right sides of the calico and the lining pieces together, overlapping the two hemmed edges slightly. Pin the cord ties in place and machine-stitch together around all four sides.
The opening at back where the hemmed edges overlap is where wadding can be inserted. Turn right side out, press and insert a piece of wadding cut to size. Slip-stitch the openings closed.

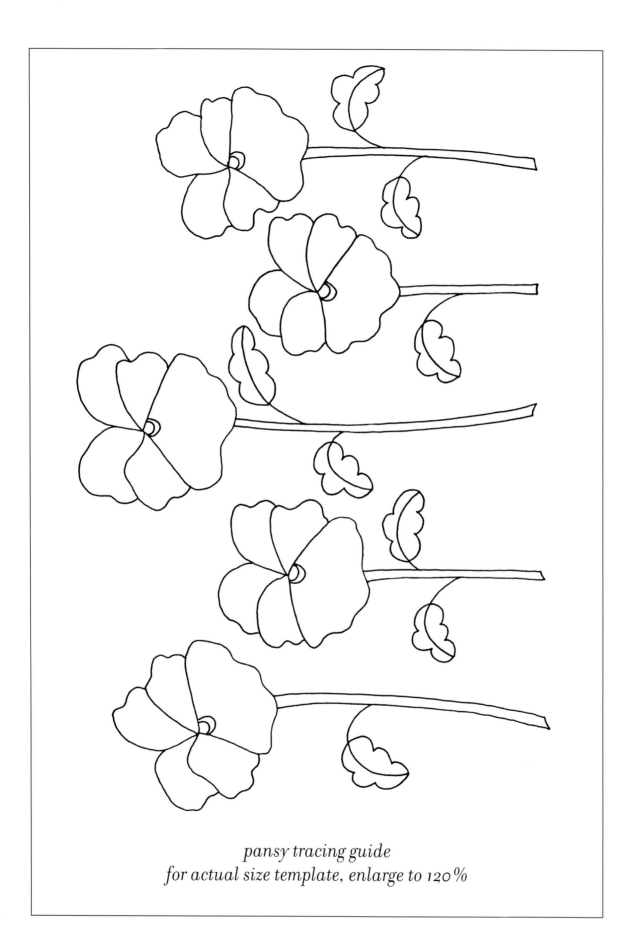

pansy tracing guide
for actual size template, enlarge to 120%

pansy
breakfast tray

MATERIALS

Wooden tray
(approx. 44 x 35 cm,
17 1/2 x 14 in)

Plaid FolkArt paint:
Lemonade, Lemon Custard,
Light Periwinkle

Plaid FolkArt Artists'
Pigment: Titanium White

Colour photocopy of
pansies, enlarged to 170%

Coarse-haired
house-painting brush

Varnishing brush

Decoupage glue

Decoupage roller

Soft cloth, moistened

Scissors

Low-tack sticky-tape

Black lead pencil

Spray waterbottle

Sandpaper, fine grade

Waterbased varnish

METHOD

Apply enough coats of Titanium White paint to achieve a good coverage over the entire tray. Sand lightly between coats. Allow to dry.

To create the soft lemon-coloured background you will need to spray the surface with a light mist of water. Pick up Lemonade and Lemon Custard on the coarse-haired brush and lightly blend on the tray's surface. Allow to dry before lightly marking a border 20 mm (3/4 in) in from the edge in pencil, and laying low-tack sticky-tape outside the line. Place another row of tape inside that line, leaving a 5 mm (1/4 in) gap. Paint the gap with two layers of Light Periwinkle. When dry, carefully peel the tape away to reveal a neat border. If any paint has seeped beneath the tape, just touch up the spots with background colour. When dry, seal with a light coat of varnish prior to gluing on the designs.

Decoupage Seal front of photocopied pansy design with varnish and when dry, carefully cut around shapes. It will be easier to cut leaves free of the leaf stalks and draw in the fine stalks later using the Artline pen. Test your arrangement of flowers before gluing, making sure the two outer pansies slightly overlap the border at the ends of the tray. Refer to the photograph for guidance.

Apply glue to the back of each pansy and press in place with fingertips. Use the decoupage roller to remove any excess glue and trapped air, being especially careful as you work along the main stems. Wipe away excess glue with a soft moistened cloth. When all flowers are glued in place, wipe the entire surface of tray again with the soft moistened cloth. Draw in leaf stalks with Artline pen.

Allow to dry overnight. Paint with several layers of varnish to protect tray.

tulips

MATERIALS

Calico,
2 x 40 cm (16 in) squares

Plaid FolkArt paint:
Lemon Custard, Cardinal
Red, Fresh Foliage, Clover

Plaid FolkArt Artists'
Pigment: Medium Yellow,
Payne's Gray

Plaid fabric medium

Brushes: 12 mm (1/2 in)
angle shader, 5 mm (1/4 in)
angle shader, No. 4 round

Black lead pencil

Tile for palette

Watertub

Hairdryer

Paper towel

Old absorbent towel

Lightbox
or other tracing system

METHOD

Wash calico once and press well to remove creases.

Overlock edges of both squares of calico, then turn over a 12 mm (1/2 in) hem and stitch by machine.

This project is outlined lightly in pencil, giving a softer appearance to the finished artwork. Using your lightbox, trace one of the tulip designs onto each serviette.

Petals Refer to the photograph for colour guidance. Work one petal at a time, drying each before moving to next area (the order you paint the petals is not important). Begin by painting the petal with fabric medium and while this is still wet, apply a wash of Lemonade. To strengthen the colour in the lower area of each petal, float in some Medium Yellow. At the tips of the petals float in some Cardinal Red, which will soften as it seeps into the middle section of the petal as long as the calico is still wet. Repeat with more Cardinal Red if more impact is required. To create the shadow area on the top inner section of one of the tulips, float in a little Payne's Grey. Paint in a float of Payne's Grey around the curved base of both tulips (this will give a more realistic 'bowl-like' effect).

Leaves and stem Begin by applying a layer of fabric medium. Then paint in a wash of Fresh Foliage to the darker leaf section. Build up shading by floating on Clover. Repeat this step until enough depth has been achieved. For the lighter-coloured turn-back of the leaf, paint in a wash of Fresh Foliage. Deepen the colour slightly at the edges and tip by floating on Fresh Foliage. For the stems, use the 5 mm (1/4 in) shader and apply a wash of Fresh Foliage. Deepen this colour at the edges by floating on more Fresh Foliage.

Assess your work and, if necessary, strengthen the shaded areas by floating on more colour.

napkins

PAINTED CALICO PROJECT

tulips
placemats

MATERIALS

2 craftwood place mats:
approx. 29 x 21 cm
(11 1/2 x 8 1/2 in)

2 craftwood coasters:
approx. 11 x 9 cm (4 1/2 x 3
1/2 in)

Plaid FolkArt paint:
Emerald Isle, Bayberry,
Metallic Inca Gold

Plaid FolkArt Artists'
Pigment: Titanium White

Colour photocopies of
tulips:
1 set copied at 100%
1 set reduced to 35%

Coarse-haired
house-painting brush

Varnishing brush

25 mm (1 in) foam
applicator

Decoupage glue

Decoupage roller

Soft cloth, moistened

Scissors

Spray waterbottle

Sandpaper, fine grade

Waterbased varnish

METHOD

Apply enough coats of Titanium White paint to achieve a good coverage to all surfaces of the placemats and coasters. Sand lightly between coats.

To create the streaked green background you will need to squeeze a few rows of Emerald Isle and Bayberry, approximately 5 mm (1/4 in) wide and 20 mm (3/4 in) apart, across the white painted surface. Use the coarse-haired brush and a light mist of water to streak the colours softly together. If necessary, repeat this step to achieve a good coverage. Allow to dry. Pick up Inca Gold metallic paint on the flat side of the foam applicator and paint the edges of placemats and coasters. When dry, seal all surfaces with a light coat of varnish prior to gluing on the designs.

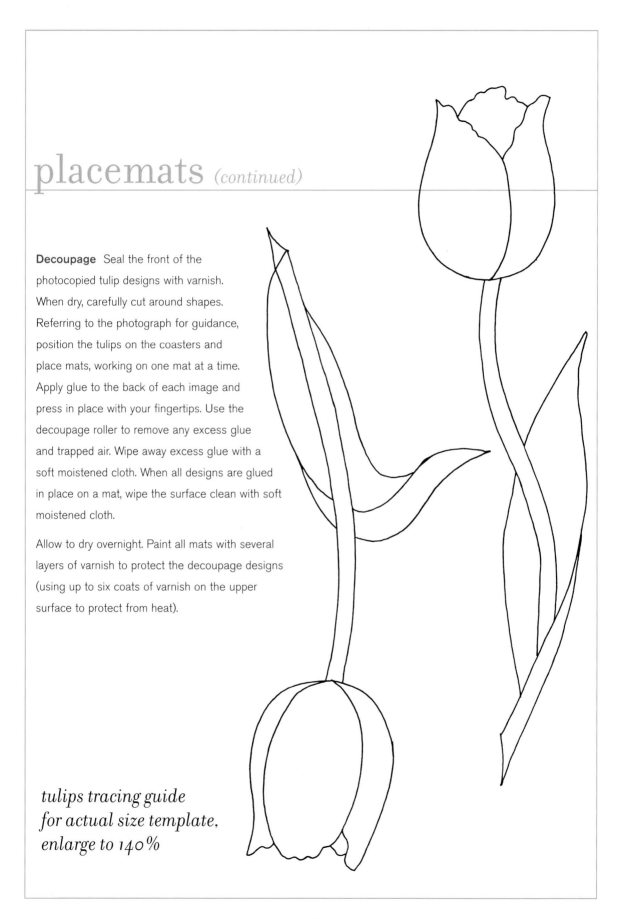

placemats *(continued)*

Decoupage Seal the front of the photocopied tulip designs with varnish. When dry, carefully cut around shapes. Referring to the photograph for guidance, position the tulips on the coasters and place mats, working on one mat at a time. Apply glue to the back of each image and press in place with your fingertips. Use the decoupage roller to remove any excess glue and trapped air. Wipe away excess glue with a soft moistened cloth. When all designs are glued in place on a mat, wipe the surface clean with soft moistened cloth.

Allow to dry overnight. Paint all mats with several layers of varnish to protect the decoupage designs (using up to six coats of varnish on the upper surface to protect from heat).

*tulips tracing guide
for actual size template,
enlarge to 140%*

daffodil

MATERIALS

Calico,
47 cm (18 ¹/₂ in) square

Yellow fabric, e.g. poplin,
for back of cushion,
50 x 115 cm (20 x 45 in)

Plaid FolkArt paint:
Lemon Custard, School Bus
Yellow, Tangerine, Bayberry,
Green Meadow

Plaid FolkArt Artists'
Pigment: Hauser Green Light,
Raw Umber, Titanium White

Plaid dimensional fabric
paint: Black Shiny

Plaid fabric medium

Brushes: 25 mm (1 in) flat,
12 mm (¹/₂ in) angle shader,
5 mm (¹/₄ in) angle shader,
No 4 round

Tile for palette

Watertub

Hairdryer

Paper towel

Old absorbent towel

Lightbox
or other tracing system

Cushion insert:
40 cm (16 in) square

Piping cord,
approx. 170 cm (67 in)

3 buttons or strip of Velcro

METHOD

Trace the outline of the daffodil onto the calico using the Black Shiny dimensional paint. The three stamens can be drawn in later when the painting is complete. Allow to dry for twelve hours, or set using the hairdryer.

Painting For the larger areas, use the 25 mm (1 in) flat brush. Vary the size of the brush you are using according to the width of the area being painted.

Petals Begin painting the petals, working one at a time and drying well before moving to the adjoining area. The order in which you work doesn't really matter, but you might prefer to do the back petals first, then the side petals, and the front ones last. Paint a layer of fabric medium into the outlined section. While this is still wet apply a soft wash of Lemon Custard. Halt the bleeding process with the hairdryer. Refer to photograph for shading details.

Build up strength of colour by floating in School Bus Yellow and Tangerine. For more impact, float a touch of Raw Umber to the inner sections of some petals, where they overlap. Once the petals are completed, paint in the trumpet of the daffodil, building up shading on the lower bowl and inner top section with School Bus Yellow and Tangerine. Float a little Raw Umber under the front fluted section and to deepen shadow at centre of flower.

Leaves Paint in a layer of fabric medium on the leaf area. Apply a wash of Hauser Green Light, then randomly, over this wash paint in Bayberry for slight colour variation in parts. The shading is done by floating in Green Meadow, intensifying the colour where the leaf is behind the stem, upper petals and under the leaf turn-back.

Stem Use the 5 mm (¹/₄ in) flat brush to paint in fabric medium, then a light wash of Hauser Green Light. Float in more depth of colour where stem joins flower, using Green Meadow.

Highlights and stamens If any areas of paintwork need highlighting, moisten the area with a little water and apply some Titanium White using the tip of the round brush.

cushion

PAINTED CALICO PROJECT

cushion *(continued)*

When all paint has dried, draw in the three black stamens at the centre of the flower with dimensional fabric paint.

Making up cushion Trim the painted calico to measure 45 cm (18 in) square. Cut two rectangles of the yellow fabric to measure 45 x 28 cm (18 x 11 in). Stitch a hem along one long edge of each. These will overlap to form an opening on the back of cushion. For piping, cut a strip of yellow fabric 8 cm (3 in) wide and 173 cm (68 in) long, joining as necessary for one continuous length. Fold piping over cord and stitch using zipper-foot on machine. Pin the piping to the cushion front around outer edge. With right sides facing, pin the two rectangles of cushion back over this, with the hemmed edges in the centre. Stitch through all layers using zipper-foot to stitch close to the piping. Turn the cover right side out and press. Sew buttons or Velcro to secure opening at back of cushion.

daffodil tracing guide
for actual size template, enlarge to 150%

daffodil
terracotta planter

MATERIALS

Terracotta pot,
approx. 18 cm (7 in) high

Plaid FolkArt paint:
Emerald Isle

Plaid FolkArt Artists'
Pigment: Titanium White

3 colour photocopies
of daffodil:
2 reduced to 42%, one of
which is reverse-copied
1 reduced to 47%

Coarse-haired
house-painting brush

Varnishing brush

Decoupage glue

Decoupage roller

Soft cloth, moistened

Scissors

Spray waterbottle

Waterbased varnish

METHOD

Apply enough coats of Titanium White paint over outer surface of pot to give a good coverage. Once dry, pick up Emerald Green on the coarse-haired brush and paint in a horizontal direction. You can spray with a mist of water to make the paint flow more freely. Allow to dry before painting with a coat of varnish.

Decoupage Seal fronts of photocopied daffodil designs with varnish and when dry, carefully cut around shapes. Apply glue to the back of each design and press in place with fingertips. Use the decoupage roller to remove any excess glue and trapped air. Wipe away excess glue with a soft moistened cloth. When all designs are glued in place, wipe the surface clean again with a soft moistened cloth.

Allow to dry overnight. Paint with several layers of varnish to protect the surface. Note that you should not plant directly into this pot, but use it to disguise a plastic pot.

iris

MATERIALS

Calico,
47 cm (18 1/2 in) square

Blue fabric, e.g. poplin,
for back of cushion,
50 x 115 cm (20 x 45 in)

Plaid FolkArt paint:
Night Sky, Brilliant Blue,
True Blue, Periwinkle,
Holly Leaf, Bayberry,
Lemon Custard

Plaid FolkArt Artists'
Pigment: Titanium White

Plaid dimensional fabric
paint: Black Shiny

Plaid fabric medium

Brushes: 25 mm (1 in) flat,
12 mm (1/2 in) angle shader,
5 mm (1/4 in) angle shader,
No. 4 round

Tile for palette

Watertub

Hairdryer

Paper towel

Old absorbent towel

Lightbox or other tracing
system

Cushion insert,
40 cm (16 in) square

Piping cord,
approx. 170 cm (67 in)

3 buttons or strip of Velcro

METHOD

Wash calico once and press well to remove creases.

Trace the outline of the iris onto the calico using the Black Shiny dimensional paint. Allow to dry for twelve hours, or set with the hairdryer.

Painting For the larger areas, use the 25 mm (1 in) flat brush. Vary the size of the brush you are using according to the width of the area being painted.

Petals Paint the petals one at a time, drying well before moving on to the next, adjoining one. Begin with the two upper petals at the back. Paint a layer of fabric medium into the outlined section. Apply fabric medium and while still wet, paint in a wash of True Blue, avoiding the small turn-back area at the top of each petal. These are painted with a mix of Periwinkle and Titanium White (1:1). Halt the bleeding process with a hairdryer. Referring to the photograph for colour variations, float in Night Sky where the petals meet the centre of the flower. Over this, float in some Periwinkle.

Referring again to the photograph, paint the three lower petals with variations of the three blues and Periwinkle. Avoid applying paint to the middle section of the front lower petal — this will create a highlight. Paint Lemon Custard on the central stamen area, adding a few fine dots of Titanium White.

Leaves Paint in fabric medium on the leaf area. Apply a wash of Holly Leaf on the lower area and Bayberry on the tips. The shading is done by floating in stronger colour with Holly Leaf. For the highlights on the leaves, moisten the area with a little water, and paint in a line of Titanium White with the No. 4 round brush, which should soften on the edges.

Stem Use the 5 mm (1/4 in) flat brush to paint in fabric medium, then a light wash of Bayberry. Add a highlight down the centre of the stem by moistening with a little water, and paint in a line of Titanium White with the No. 4 round brush.

cushion

PAINTED CALICO PROJECT

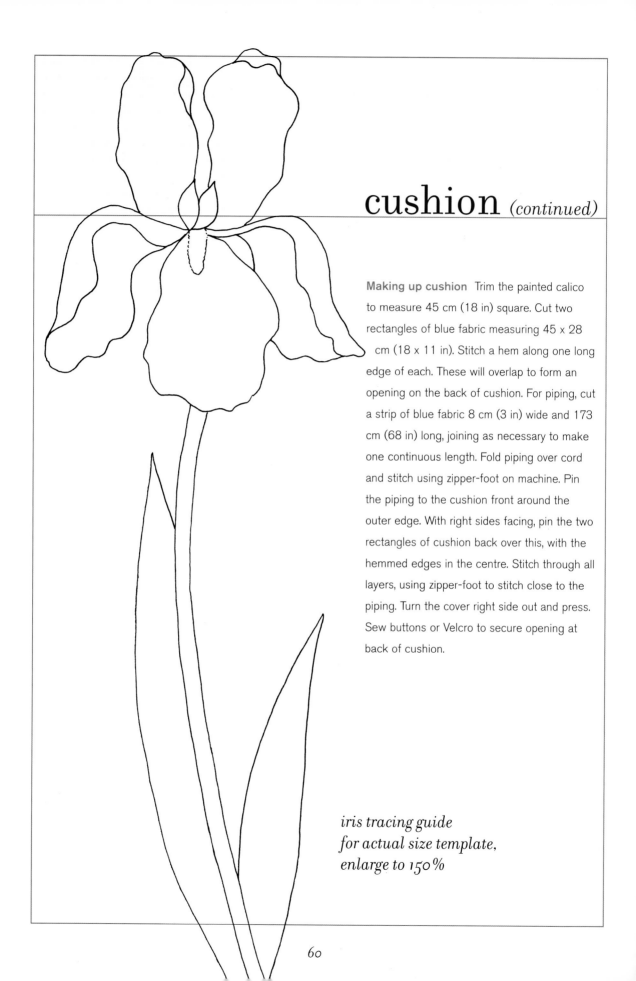

cushion *(continued)*

Making up cushion Trim the painted calico to measure 45 cm (18 in) square. Cut two rectangles of blue fabric measuring 45 x 28 cm (18 x 11 in). Stitch a hem along one long edge of each. These will overlap to form an opening on the back of cushion. For piping, cut a strip of blue fabric 8 cm (3 in) wide and 173 cm (68 in) long, joining as necessary to make one continuous length. Fold piping over cord and stitch using zipper-foot on machine. Pin the piping to the cushion front around the outer edge. With right sides facing, pin the two rectangles of cushion back over this, with the hemmed edges in the centre. Stitch through all layers, using zipper-foot to stitch close to the piping. Turn the cover right side out and press. Sew buttons or Velcro to secure opening at back of cushion.

iris tracing guide
for actual size template,
enlarge to 150%

iris
greeting card

MATERIALS

Colour photocopy of iris, reduced to 54%

Sheet of blue paper

Heavy-weight copying paper

Scissors

Decoupage glue

Decoupage roller

Low-tack sticky-tape, double-sided

Ruler

Knitting needle

METHOD

Trim the photocopied iris design to leave a rectangle measuring approximately 11 x 21 cm (4 1/4 x 8 1/4 in). Use the double-sided sticky-tape to attach the design to one side of the blue backing paper, leaving a 15 mm (5/8 in) border on the right-hand edge. Have the mounted design photocopied again onto heavy-weight paper.

Work out how wide you want the card to be and place a ruler along the fold line. Run the pointed end of a knitting needle down this line to form a groove. This will make it easier to fold the card. Fold card along this groove and cut off any excess. Make as many copies as needed. Keep the mounted design in case you want to make more copies later on. You could copy the other three cushion designs in this manner to make a gift set, as shown in the photograph. You might consider changing the backing colour to vary the effect.

daisy

Calico,
47 cm (18 ½ in) square

Bright pink fabric, e.g. poplin,
for back of cushion,
50 x 115 cm (20 x 45 in)

Plaid FolkArt paint:
Light Fuchsia, Magenta,
Bayberry, Leaf Green,
Hunter Green, Yellow Lemon

Plaid FolkArt Artists'
Pigment: Burnt Umber,
Titanium White

Plaid dimensional fabric
paint: Black Shiny

Plaid fabric medium

Brushes: 25 mm (1 in) flat,
12 mm (½ in) angle shader,
5 mm (¼ in) angle shader,
No. 4 round

Tile for palette

Watertub

Hairdryer

Paper towel

Old absorbent towel

Lightbox
or other tracing system

Cushion insert,
40 cm (16 in) square

Piping cord,
approx. 170 cm (67 in)

3 buttons or strip of Velcro

METHOD

Wash calico once and press well to remove creases.

Trace the outline of the daisy onto the calico using the Black Shiny dimensional paint. Allow to dry for twelve hours, or set with the hairdryer.

Painting For the larger areas, use the 25 mm (1 in) flat brush. Vary the size of the brush you are using according to the width of the area being painted.

Petals Paint the petals one at a time, allowing each area to dry well before moving to the adjoining area. Paint a layer of fabric medium into the outlined area before using a wash of Light Fuchsia. Halt the bleeding process with a hairdryer. Try to make the lower petals slightly deeper in colour. Next to the yellow centre, float in stronger colour, using a little Magenta blended on the edge of your angled shader.

Yellow centre Paint with fabric medium, then a wash of Lemon Yellow. Float in deeper shading at the lower edge using Burnt Umber. Use the round brush to pick up Lemon Yellow on the tip and pad this in over entire centre area. This will build up a textured appearance. Repeat the process, using Titanium White at the top and Burnt Umber at the base.

Leaves Paint fabric medium into the leaf area and apply a light wash of Leaf Green. Shade by floating in stronger colour on one side of each leaf using Hunter Green. On the other side of leaf, shade with Bayberry. Use the fine tip of the round brush to lightly paint in the centre line on each leaf in Hunter Green.

Stem Use the 5 mm (¼ in) flat brush to paint in fabric medium, then a light wash of Leaf Green. Shade on one side using Hunter Green; on the other side use Bayberry. Build up extra shading at the top of stem where it meets the daisy.

cushion

cushion *(continued)*

Making up cushion Trim the painted calico to measure 45 cm (18 in) square. Cut two rectangles of pink fabric 45 cm x 28 cm (18 x 11 in). Stitch a hem along one long edge of each. These will overlap to form an opening on the back of cushion. For piping, cut a strip of pink fabric 8 cm (3 in) wide and 173 cm (68 in) long, joining as necessary to make one continuous length. Fold piping over cord and stitch using zipper-foot on machine. Pin the piping to the cushion front around outer edge. With right sides facing, pin the two rectangles of cushion back over this, with the hemmed edges in the centre. Stitch through all layers, using zipper-foot to stitch close to the piping. Turn the cover right side out and press. Sew buttons or Velcro to secure opening at back of cushion.

daisy tracing guide
for actual size template, enlarge to 150%

daisy
papier-mâché boxes

MATERIALS

¹/₂

2 oval papier-mâché boxes:

1 approx. 29 cm x 21 cm (11 1/2 x 8 1/4 in)

1 approx. 21 cm x 15 cm (8 1/4 x 6 in)

Plaid FolkArt paint: True Blue, Light Fuchsia

Plaid FolkArt Artists' Pigment: Titanium White

4 colour photocopies of daisy:

2 reduced to 80%

2 reduced to 58%

Base-coating brush

Varnishing brush

Decoupage glue

Decoupage roller

Soft cloth, moistened

Scissors

Waterbased varnish

METHOD

Apply enough coats of Titanium White over inner and outer surfaces of boxes to achieve a good coverage. Allow to dry. Use the base-coating brush to apply True Blue paint in criss-cross strokes over the outer surface of both boxes. Wash the brush and paint the insides of the boxes with Light Fuchsia, also in criss-cross fashion. Allow to dry before painting all surfaces with a coat of varnish. Allow to dry before gluing on daisy designs.

Decoupage Seal fronts of photocopied daisies with varnish and when dry, carefully cut around shapes. Apply glue to the back of each design and press in place with your fingertips on the lids of the boxes. Use decoupage roller to remove any excess glue and trapped air. Wipe away excess glue with a soft moistened cloth. When all designs are glued in place, wipe the surface clean again, with soft moistened cloth. Allow to dry overnight. Apply several coats of varnish to all outer surfaces.

poppy

Calico,
48 cm (18 ½ in) square

Orange fabric, e.g. poplin,
for back of cushion,
50 x 115 cm (20 x 45 in)

Plaid FolkArt paint:
Tangerine, Clover, Green
Meadow, Lime Yellow

Plaid FolkArt Artists'
Pigment: Pure Orange,
Red Light, Medium Yellow,
Hauser Green Light,
Burnt Umber

Plaid dimensional fabric
paint: Black Shiny

Plaid fabric medium

Brushes: 25 mm (1 in) flat,
12 mm (½ in) angle shader,
5 mm (¼ in) angle shader,
No. 4 round, fine liner

Tile for palette

Watertub

Hairdryer

Paper towel

Old absorbent towel

Lightbox
or other tracing system

Cushion insert
40 cm (16 in) square

Piping cord,
approx. 170 cm (67 in)

3 buttons or strip of Velcro

METHOD

Wash calico once and press well to remove creases.

Trace the outline of the poppy onto the calico using the Black Shiny dimensional paint. Allow to dry 12 hours, or set with the hairdryer.

Painting For the larger areas, use the 25 mm (1 in) flat brush. Vary the size of the brush you are using according to the width of the area being painted.

Petals Begin with the upper back petal, first painting a layer of fabric medium into the outlined section. While still wet, paint with a wash of Tangerine. Build up strength of colour near the centre of poppy by floating in Pure Orange. Repeat this step for all petals (except for turn-backs on side petals). Add a float of Red Light near the centre on the two side petals. At the base of the front petal, float in Burnt Umber to create a shadow where the petal would curve underneath. Paint the two turn-backs of the side petals in Tangerine.

Centre Paint with a wash of Hauser Green Light and shade at the base with Green Meadow. Allow to dry before using the fine liner brush to paint in the 6 fine lines in Lime Yellow. Dry the calico well in this area and use the fine tip of the liner brush to paint in the stamens in Medium Yellow, referring to the photograph for placement.

Leaves and bud Paint in fabric medium on the leaves. Apply a wash of Hauser Green Light to the leaves, keeping the middle section quite pale in colour as a highlight. To shade around the outer edges, float a stronger wash of Hauser Green Light to the top edge of each leaf, and float Green Meadow around the fluted lower edges.

Apply fabric medium to the bud and then a wash of Hauser Green Light with a touch of Clover. Leave the middle area quite pale as a highlight. Strengthen the colour around the curved lower edge by floating in Green Meadow. Pick up some diluted Clover on the tip of the fine liner brush and paint in the centre line of the bud. This line will soften slightly if the base fabric is still a little wet.

cushion

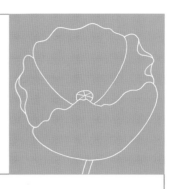

PAINTED CALICO PROJECT

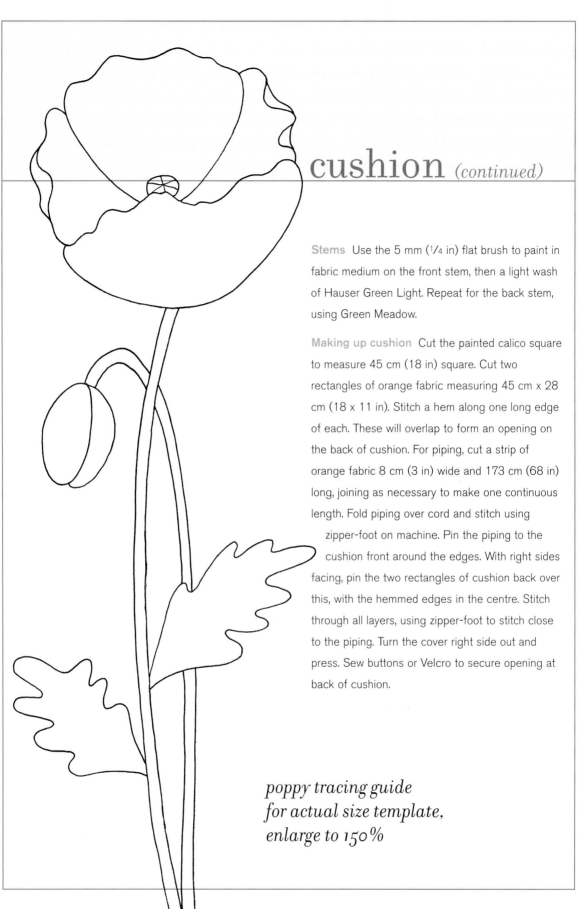

cushion *(continued)*

Stems Use the 5 mm (1/4 in) flat brush to paint in fabric medium on the front stem, then a light wash of Hauser Green Light. Repeat for the back stem, using Green Meadow.

Making up cushion Cut the painted calico square to measure 45 cm (18 in) square. Cut two rectangles of orange fabric measuring 45 cm x 28 cm (18 x 11 in). Stitch a hem along one long edge of each. These will overlap to form an opening on the back of cushion. For piping, cut a strip of orange fabric 8 cm (3 in) wide and 173 cm (68 in) long, joining as necessary to make one continuous length. Fold piping over cord and stitch using zipper-foot on machine. Pin the piping to the cushion front around the edges. With right sides facing, pin the two rectangles of cushion back over this, with the hemmed edges in the centre. Stitch through all layers, using zipper-foot to stitch close to the piping. Turn the cover right side out and press. Sew buttons or Velcro to secure opening at back of cushion.

poppy tracing guide
for actual size template,
enlarge to 150%

poppy
document holder

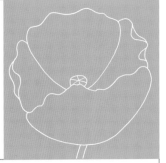

DÉCOUPAGE PROJECT

MATERIALS

Craftwood document holder, approx. 38 x 28 x 12 cm (15 x 11 x 4 3/4 in)

Plaid FolkArt Artists' Pigment: Pure Black, Pure Orange, Titanium White

3 colour photocopies of poppy, reduced to 70%

Basecoating brush

Varnishing brush

Decoupage glue

Decoupage roller

Soft cloth, moistened

Scissors

Spray waterbottle

Sandpaper, fine grade

Waterbased varnish

METHOD

Remove hinges from document holder to make painting easier.

Apply several coats of Pure Black paint over all surfaces of document holder (except for the upper and lower border---refer to photograph). Paint the border areas with a coat of Titanium White, allow to dry and sand lightly, then apply two coats of Pure Orange.

Apply a coat of varnish to the front of the lid before beginning the decoupage. Seal fronts of photocopied poppies with varnish and when dry, carefully cut around shapes. Check correct placement on lid before applying glue to the back of each design and pressing in place with fingertips.

Due to the length of this design, it will be easier to glue the flowers and stems separately. Cut the poppy flower away from the stem and reassemble the design as you glue the pieces in place.

Use the decoupage roller to remove any excess glue and trapped air. Wipe away excess glue with a soft moistened cloth. When all designs are glued in place, wipe the surface clean again, with soft moistened cloth.

Allow to dry overnight. To complete the project, paint all surfaces with several coats of varnish.

flower bear

MATERIALS

Craftwood or wooden frame, internal dimensions approx. 25 x 20 cm (10 x 8 in)

Calico, 34 x 36 cm (13 1/2 x 14 1/4 in)

Quilt wadding cut to internal dimensions of frame

Plaid FolkArt paint: Nutmeg, French Vanilla, Light Periwinkle, Holly Leaf, Lemon Custard, Brilliant Blue, Fresh Foliage

Plaid FolkArt Artists' Pigment: Titanium White, Burnt Umber

Brushes: 12 mm (1/2 in) angle shader, No. 1 round

Black Artline pen No. 5

Black lead pencil

Tile for palette

Watertub

Hairdryer

Paper towel

Old absorbent towel

Lightbox or other tracing system

Masking tape

METHOD

Trace the bear design onto calico (very lightly with black lead pencil).

It is particularly important with this design to work on one individual area and dry it with the hairdryer before beginning the next area.

Begin by moistening the area on calico with a wash of water. This will help to achieve a more even colour when the paint wash is applied.

On your palette mix Nutmeg and Titanium White (1:1) and then add enough water to make an ink-like consistency. Using the 12 mm (1/2 in) angle shader and the colour floating technique (see page 13), use the paint mixture to apply a waterwash over each section of the bear. Leave the flower, leaf and mouth areas free of paint.

Refer to the photograph and build up shading at the base of the ears using straight Nutmeg. For stronger shading use Burnt Umber. Shade the areas at the tops of the legs, under the chin and around the arms.

The background for the nose/mouth area is painted with French Vanilla. Apply this as solid paint rather than a waterwash.

Daisy Paint the petals with a wash of Light Periwinkle, then add shading with Brilliant Blue. Use Lemon Custard to paint the centre of daisy. Pick up some Titanium White on the tip of the round brush and add a couple of highlights to petals and flower centre.

Paint leaves with a wash of Fresh Foliage, with extra shading at base of leaves using Holly Leaf. The stem and the centre lines on the leaves can be painted with Holly Leaf on the tip of the round brush.

Face details When all paintwork is dry, lay the painted calico over the design with a light source behind and using a pencil very lightly draw in the eyes, nose and mouth. Then go over the pencil lines with the Artline pen, filling in the eyes and nose. Add a highlight to each eye using Titanium White on the tip of the round brush.

framed

PAINTED CALICO PROJECT

flower bear framed *(continued)*

For the stitching lines above eyes and on body, use Nutmeg with a touch of water and paint in with the round brush.

Framing Paint frame with two coats of Titanium White. When dry, dry-brush with Light Periwinkle, following the line of the frame with your brushstrokes. Coat with varnish when dry. Place quilt wadding over the backing board and fold the painted calico over the backing, centring the bear. Secure at the back with masking tape. Position in frame and press metal clips down to hold.

flower bear tracing guide
for actual size template,
enlarge to 120%

flower bear
blackboard

MATERIALS

Craftwood blackboard,
45 x 60 cm (18 x 24 in)

5 wooden daisy shapes,
approx. 6.5 cm (2 1/2 in) high

Plaid FolkArt Paint:
Lemon Custard, Buttercup,
Light Periwinkle, True Blue

Plaid FolkArt Artists'
Pigment: Titanium White

7 colour photocopies
of bear:
3 copies at 100%
4 copies reduced to 70%

Basecoating brush

Varnishing brush

25 mm (1 in)
foam applicator

Decoupage glue

Wood glue

Decoupage roller

Soft cloth, moistened

Scissors

Waterspray bottle

Sandpaper, fine grade

Waterbased varnish

METHOD

Remove blackboard section from frame and set aside. Apply several coats of Titanium White over all sides of frame. Sand lightly before applying a final topcoat of Buttercup and Lemon Custard, using the basecoating brush to blend these two colours together slightly over the front of frame in straight lines, following direction of frame. Paint the back of the frame in Lemon Custard. Use the flat edge of the foam applicator to apply a mix of Light Periwinkle and True Blue (1:1) to the edge of the frame. When dry, paint frame with a coat of varnish.

Wooden daisies Paint each daisy with several coats of Light Periwinkle and True Blue (1:1). When dry, print the yellow centre circles with the flat base of the foam applicator, using Lemon Custard. Paint with varnish and set aside.

Decoupage Seal the fronts of the photocopied bears with varnish and when dry, carefully cut around shapes. Refer to the photograph for correct placement, cutting some of the smaller bears to allow you to use the upper and lower sections separately. Apply glue to the back of each design and press in place with fingertips. Use the decoupage roller to remove any excess glue and trapped air. Wipe away excess glue with a soft moistened cloth. When all designs are glued in place, wipe the surface clean again with the soft moistened cloth. When dry, apply several coats of varnish and dry overnight. Glue the daisies in place using wood glue and replace the blackboard insert.

see over for photograph

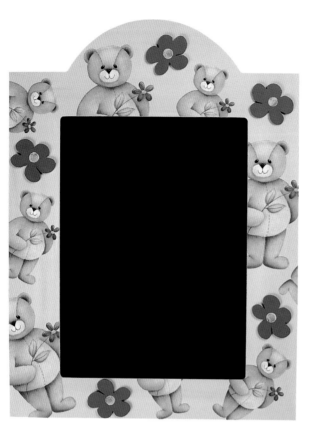

note: the toybox découpage project uses photocopies of both the flower bear and the ballet bear

bears
toybox

MATERIALS

Wooden toy-box [[size??]]

[[Libby, please add measurements as author has not kept record]]

Plaid FolkArt Paint: Periwinkle, Light Fuchsia

Plaid FolkArt glazing medium

Watercolour paper, 22 x 42 cm (8 ³/₄ x 16 ¹/₂ in)

3 colour photocopies of bear with flower:
2 at 100%
(1 reverse-copied)
1 reduced to 50%
2 colour photocopies of ballet bear:
1 at 100%
1 reduced to 50%

Basecoating brush

Varnishing brush

Wood glue

Decoupage glue

Decoupage roller

Soft cloth

Soft cloth, moistened

Scissors

Spray waterbottle

Low-tack sticky-tape, double-sided

Waterbased varnish

METHOD

Remove the hinges from the toy-box to make painting easier. Make a mix of equal parts glaze medium and Periwinkle. Working on one surface at a time, paint glaze mixture over toy-box with the basecoating brush. Wipe over with a soft cloth to work the mixture into the timber surface. Repeat until entire project is painted. The woodgrain will be visible through the tinted glaze. Photocopy the bears from the original painted calico and cut out.

Divide the watercolour paper into three rectangles measuring approximately 22 x 14 cm (8 ³/₄ x 5 ¹/₂ in). Paint two of the pieces in Periwinkle and the other in Light Fuchsia. Spray a light mist of water on the paper and apply light strokes of paint with the base-coating brush, making the paint slightly darker in parts to give a grained effect. These different coloured background papers will be interchanged during the final photocopying process.

Attach the three large cut-out bears to the background papers with double-sided sticky-tape, the two mirror-image flower bears on the blue backgrounds and the ballet bear on the pink background. Photocopy at 100% to give you three images for the top of the toy-box. Seal the fronts of the designs with a coat of varnish and when dry, use a straight-edge and a craft knife to cut a rectangle around each bear measuring 20.5 x 13 cm (8 x 5 ¹/₄ in).

Now detach the large bears from the backgrounds and attach the smaller bears (referring to the photograph for colour combinations) and photocopy at 100%. You will need five bears for the front of the box and six for the sides (eleven in total). Seal the fronts of the designs with a coat of varnish and when dry, use a straight-edge and a craft knife to cut a rectangle around each bear measuring 10.25 x 6.5 cm (4 x 2 ¹/₂ in).

Apply glue to the back of each rectangle and press in place with fingertips. Use the decoupage roller to remove any excess glue and trapped air. Wipe away excess glue with a soft moistened cloth. When all designs are glued in place, wipe the surface clean again, with soft moistened cloth. When dry, apply several coats of varnish over toy-box and dry overnight.

ballet bear

Craftwood or wooden frame, internal dimensions approx. 25 x 20 cm (10 x 8 in)

Calico, 34 x 36 cm (13 1/2 x 14 1/4 in)

Quilt wadding cut to internal dimensions of frame

Plaid FolkArt paint: Nutmeg, French Vanilla, Light Fuchsia, Magenta

Plaid FolkArt Artists' Pigment: Titanium White, Burnt Umber

Brushes: 12 mm (1/2 in) angle shader, No. 1 round

Black Artline pen No. 5

Black lead pencil

Tile for palette

Watertub

Hairdryer

Paper towel

Old absorbent towel

Lightbox or other tracing system

Masking tape

METHOD

Trace the bear design onto calico (very lightly with black lead pencil).

It is particularly important with this design to work on one individual area and dry it with the hairdryer before beginning the next area.

Begin by moistening the area on calico with a wash of water. This will help to achieve a more even colour when the paint wash is applied.

On your palette mix Nutmeg and Titanium White (1:1) and then add enough water to make an ink-like consistency. Using the 12 mm (1/2 in) angle shader and the colour floating technique (see page 13), use this mixture to apply a waterwash over each section of the bear. Leave the ballet skirt area free of paint. Refer to the photograph and build up shading at the base of the ears using straight Nutmeg. For stronger shading use Burnt Umber. Shade the areas at top of legs, under the chin and arm areas.

The background for the nose/mouth area is painted with French Vanilla. Apply this as solid paint rather than a waterwash.

Ballet skirt and bow

Skirt Apply a wash of paint to skirt area using Light Fuchsia. Strengthen colour at waist with Magenta. Use either Light Fuchsia or Magenta on the tip of the round brush to paint in lines indicating the gathering on the skirt. Paint in wavy lines at hem of skirt using Magenta and Titanium White. Add a few highlight lines on waistband with Titanium White.

Bow Apply a wash of Light Fuchsia. Build up shading with Magenta and add highlights with Titanium White.

76

ballet bear framed *(continued)*

Face details When all paintwork is dry, lay the painted calico over the design with a light source behind and using a pencil very lightly draw in the eyes, nose and mouth. Then go over the pencil lines with the Artline pen, filling in the eyes and nose. Add a highlight to each eye using Titanium White on the tip of the round brush.

For the stitching lines above the eyes and on the body, use Nutmeg with a touch of water and paint in with the round brush.

Framing Paint frame with two coats of Titanium White.

When dry, dry-brush with Light Fuchsia, following line of frame with brush strokes. Coat with varnish when dry.

Place quilt wadding over the backing board and fold painted calico bear design over the top of backing. Secure at the back with masking tape. Replace back into frame and press metal clips down to hold.

ballet bear tracing guide
for actual size template, enlarge to 120%

suppliers

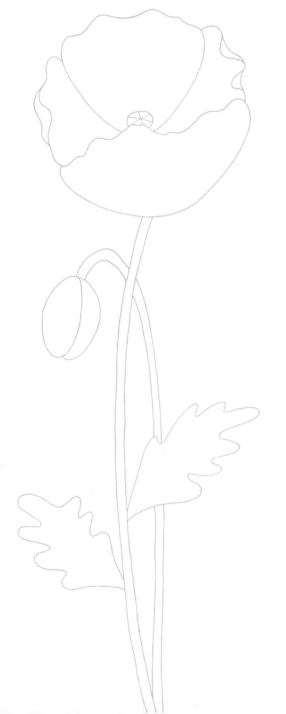

Kaisercraft Pty Ltd
PO Box 339
Belmont Vic 3216 Australia
Phone: 61 3 5240 2000
http://www.kaisercraft.com.au
Stockists of lazy susan, tissue box, oval platter,
square mirror, placemat and coasters, blackboard

Timber Turn
63 Boothby Street
Panorama SA 5041 Australia
Phone: 61 8 8266 5056
Stockists of toy-box

Spotlight Stores Pty Ltd
Head office: 100 Market Street
South Melbourne Vic 3205 Australia
Phone: 61 3 9690 8899
Stockists of paints, fabric paint, calico,
papier-mâché boxes, tray

M. Dee Agencies
2 Forster Street
Ridleyton SA 5008 Australia
Phone: 61 8 8340 3553
Stockists of document holder